DOGS SET X

AUSTRALIAN SHEPHERDS

Megan M. Gunderson
ABDO Publishing Company

visit us at
www.abdopublishing.com

Published by ABDO Publishing Company, PO Box 398166, Minneapolis, MN 55439.
Copyright © 2013 by Abdo Consulting Group, Inc. International copyrights reserved
in all countries. No part of this book may be reproduced in any form without written
permission from the publisher. The Checkerboard Library™ is a trademark and logo of
ABDO Publishing Company.

Printed in the United States of America, North Mankato, Minnesota.
102012
012013

 PRINTED ON RECYCLED PAPER

Cover Photo: Superstock
Interior Photos: Alamy pp. 7, 11; Getty Images p. 9; iStockphoto p. 5;
    Photo Researchers p. 17; Superstock p. 19; Thinkstock pp. 9, 13, 15, 20–21

Editors: Tamara L. Britton, Stephanie Hedlund
Art Direction: Neil Klinepier

Cataloging-in-Publication Data

Gunderson, Megan M., 1981-
 Australian shepherds / Megan M. Gunderson.
   p. cm. -- (Dogs)
Includes bibliographical references and index.
ISBN 978-1-61783-588-9
1. Australian shepherd dog--Juvenile literature. 2. Dogs--Juvenile literature. I. Title.
636.737--dc23
                                                                    2012946330

CONTENTS

THE DOG FAMILY

Dogs and humans have been companions for 12,000 years. Today, there are more than 78 million pet dogs in the United States alone. It's no wonder there are so many. People love **breeds** like the intelligent Australian shepherd!

Aussies are animated and **agile**. These hard workers are expert herders. And the beautiful coloring of their fur just adds to their appeal.

Like all dogs, Australian shepherds belong to the family **Canidae**. Wolves belong to this family, too. In fact, scientists believe dogs descended from the gray wolf. Early dogs helped protect people from predators. Over time, humans developed different breeds to perform a wide range of jobs.

Australian shepherds love their families, but they are reserved around new people.

Today, there are more than 400 dog **breeds** to choose from. Some are built for herding, like the Australian shepherd. Others are best suited to hunting or guarding. Still others simply make excellent companions for their owners.

AUSTRALIAN SHEPHERDS

Are Australian shepherds originally from Australia? Most people don't think so. In the 1800s, **Basque** shepherds left Australia for the United States. They brought dogs with them that had originally come from Europe. These dogs developed into the Australian shepherd **breed**.

Australian shepherds began as expert farm and ranch dogs. Today, they have additional jobs. Aussies work as guide dogs and therapy dogs. They help sniff out drugs. And, they perform search-and-rescue missions.

The **American Kennel Club (AKC)** recognized the Australian shepherd **breed** in 1991. Aussies are part of the AKC's herding group. Other dogs in this group include border collies, Shetland sheepdogs, and Welsh corgis.

Over time, these dogs have been called Spanish shepherds, pastor dogs, bob-tails, New Mexican shepherds, and California shepherds.

What They're Like

The Australian shepherd lives to work. It was **bred** for herding and guarding. It still loves these jobs today. In fact, an Aussie will try to herd children by nipping at their heels! Still, it is very tolerant of kids. If well **socialized**, an Aussie will also get along with other animals.

Ranchers love that Aussies are easy to train. Yet even city dogs can show off their natural abilities. Herding trials offer Aussies a chance to develop and showcase their talents.

Aussies also excel at **agility** trials. For these, Aussies get to prove how coordinated and smart they

are. Flyball and flying disc competitions are also fun for this **breed**. Chasing tennis balls or Frisbees is an exciting way to display speed and **agility**.

COAT AND COLOR

The Australian shepherd's weather resistant coat is perfect for a working dog. The coat is thick, but the undercoat varies with the season. It is thinner in warmer weather. These dogs **shed**!

The Aussie's fur is straight to wavy. It is moderately coarse and medium in length. There is feathering on the rear end and the backs of the front legs. The head and ears feature short, smooth hair. Male Aussies have a more prominent mane and frill.

Australian shepherds sport a beautiful range of colors. They can be blue **merle**, black, red merle, or red. They may have white or tan markings, too. If your Aussie has a merle coat, it will become darker with age.

Blue merles and blacks have black noses.
Red merles and reds have brown noses.

SIZE

Australian shepherds are medium-sized dogs. They are slightly longer than they are tall. Males are 20 to 23 inches (51 to 58 cm) tall. Females are slightly smaller. They measure 18 to 21 inches (46 to 53 cm) from paw pads to shoulders.

On average, male Aussies weigh 45 to 60 pounds (20 to 27 kg). Females usually weigh between 35 and 45 pounds (16 and 20 kg).

Strong, straight legs support the Aussie's muscular body. A deep chest reaches down to the dog's elbows. A straight back leads to a straight tail. The tail is naturally docked, so it is no more than four inches (10 cm) long.

The Aussie's head features triangular, slightly rounded ears. The ears tip forward. The Aussie's

The Aussie's striking eyes are one of its most well-known features.

almond-shaped eyes show off a keen, friendly expression. They can be brown, blue, or amber. Some also have flecks or marbling in those colors. The **muzzle** tapers to a brown or black nose.

CARE

Most dogs need exercise to stay healthy. But Aussies need a lot! This **breed** will appreciate walks, but a jog is even better for adults. Take time to get your Aussie used to water. Then it will love to go for a swim! Playing catch is great fun, too.

An Australian shepherd's coat requires weekly brushing. Be sure to check for **mats**, especially behind the ears and in the armpits. This is also a good time to make sure your dog's ears are clean.

Your pet will need a bath every three to four months. Working dogs and those that spend lots of time outside may need a bath more often. Prevent dental problems by brushing your Aussie's teeth. Do this at least once or twice a week. And, carefully trim your dog's nails every one to two weeks.

Regular visits to the veterinarian will prevent many illnesses in your Aussie. The veterinarian will provide **vaccines**. And, he or she will **spay** or **neuter** dogs that are not going to be **bred**.

FEEDING

A proper diet gives you healthy skin and strong bones. The same is true for your Aussie. Choose a commercial dog food that fits your dog's age, activity level, and taste. Be sure to read the label. Meat should be one of the first ingredients listed.

Commercial foods are designed to give your dog just the right **nutrition**. Adding people food adds extra things they may not need. And some people foods are not safe for dogs.

Proper nutrition is especially important for puppies. Aussies grow fastest during their first year of life. Puppies should be fed three to four times a day. Between six months and one year old, Aussies can switch to eating twice a day.

Fresh water should always be available, especially at mealtimes.

THINGS THEY NEED

Provide your Aussie with its own space in your home. A crate works well. Be sure it is big enough that your pet can stand up, turn around, and lie comfortably. Provide a soft pad and a blanket to make it especially cozy.

Australian shepherds love to chew. So be sure to have safe toys for them to play with. Sturdy food and water bowls are a must for the same reason.

Australian shepherds do best with lightweight nylon or leather buckle collars. Your dog's collar should include license and identification tags. If your dog gets lost, this provides vital information to the person who finds it.

Aussies love to run and play!

PUPPIES

Have you decided to make room in your home for an Australian shepherd? The next step is to find a reputable **breeder**. A good breeder wants his or her puppies to lead healthy, happy lives. So, be prepared to answer questions about the life and home you will provide for your pet.

Dogs are **pregnant** for about 63 days. Mother Australian shepherds have 5 to 8 puppies in a **litter**. Puppies can see and hear after 2 to 3 weeks. They start eating solid food around 6 weeks. By 8 to 12 weeks, your puppy will be ready to go home with you.

At home, continue **socializing** your puppy. This will help prevent unwelcome behaviors later on. And, it's a great opportunity to show off your cute new puppy! Your Australian shepherd will be a loyal companion for 11 to 15 years.

Be sure to choose a healthy puppy from a clean home. Your puppy should be friendly and interested in you!

GLOSSARY

agile - able to move quickly and easily. Agility is a sport in which a handler leads a dog through an obstacle course during a timed race.

American Kennel Club (AKC) - an organization that studies and promotes interest in purebred dogs.

Basque (BASK) - relating to a group of people from an area in northern Spain and southwestern France.

breed - a group of animals sharing the same ancestors and appearance. A breeder is a person who raises animals. Raising animals is often called breeding them.

Canidae (KAN-uh-dee) - the scientific Latin name for the dog family. Members of this family are called canids. They include wolves, jackals, foxes, coyotes, and domestic dogs.

litter - all of the puppies born at one time to a mother dog.

mat - a tangled mass.

merle - having dark patches of color on a lighter background.

muzzle - an animal's nose and jaws.

neuter (NOO-tuhr) - to remove a male animal's reproductive glands.

nutrition - that which promotes growth, provides energy, repairs body tissues, and maintains life.

pregnant - having one or more babies growing within the body.

shed - to cast off hair, feathers, skin, or other coverings or parts by a natural process.

socialize - to adapt an animal to behaving properly around people or other animals in various settings.

spay - to remove a female animal's reproductive organs.

vaccine (vak-SEEN) - a shot given to prevent illness or disease.

WEB SITES

To learn more about Australian shepherds, visit ABDO Publishing Company online. Web sites about Australian shepherds are featured on our Book Links page. These links are routinely monitored and updated to provide the most current information available.

www.abdopublishing.com

23

INDEX